MANDALA ZEN

CreativeColoringBooksForAdults.com

MandaLove Press

Hours of relaxation and calm inside ...

The simple act of coloring is being used the world over to relax, de-stress, and elevate mood. In addition to having therapeutic healing properties, coloring is just plain fun! New worlds open when you set your inner artist free!

MandaLove Press is proud to bring you **MANDALA ZEN**, a beautiful collection of 100 mandalas designed with you in mind. In this rich assortment of coloring pages, we offer everything from simple to complex.

Gather your coloring pencils, settle into an easy chair with a cup of tea, and pick a page from **MANDALA ZEN**. Let your imagination lead you into the world of color and away from the tension and stress of the day.

Our stunning designs are guaranteed to bring you many hours of bliss. Enjoy!

The MANDALA ZEN Collection is gorgeous! Get one today for you and a friend!

The mandala designs in **MANDALA ZEN** are printed one to a page, but markers can bleed through even the best paper. Two blotter pages have been added to the back of the book for you to use to keep your artwork pristine.

Free coloring pages ...

Subscribe to our newsletter today and we'll send you a free bonus set of mandalas to color. You'll also have a chance to win a brand new coloring book!
We choose a new winner every month:
http://CreativeColoringBooksForAdults.SubscribeMeNow.com/

Join us on Facebook and you'll have access to free coloring pages and more chances to win free coloring supplies and coloring books:
https://www.Facebook.com/CreativeColoringBooks

Look for our coloring books on Amazon and at your local bookstore!

Thank you for supporting independent artists!

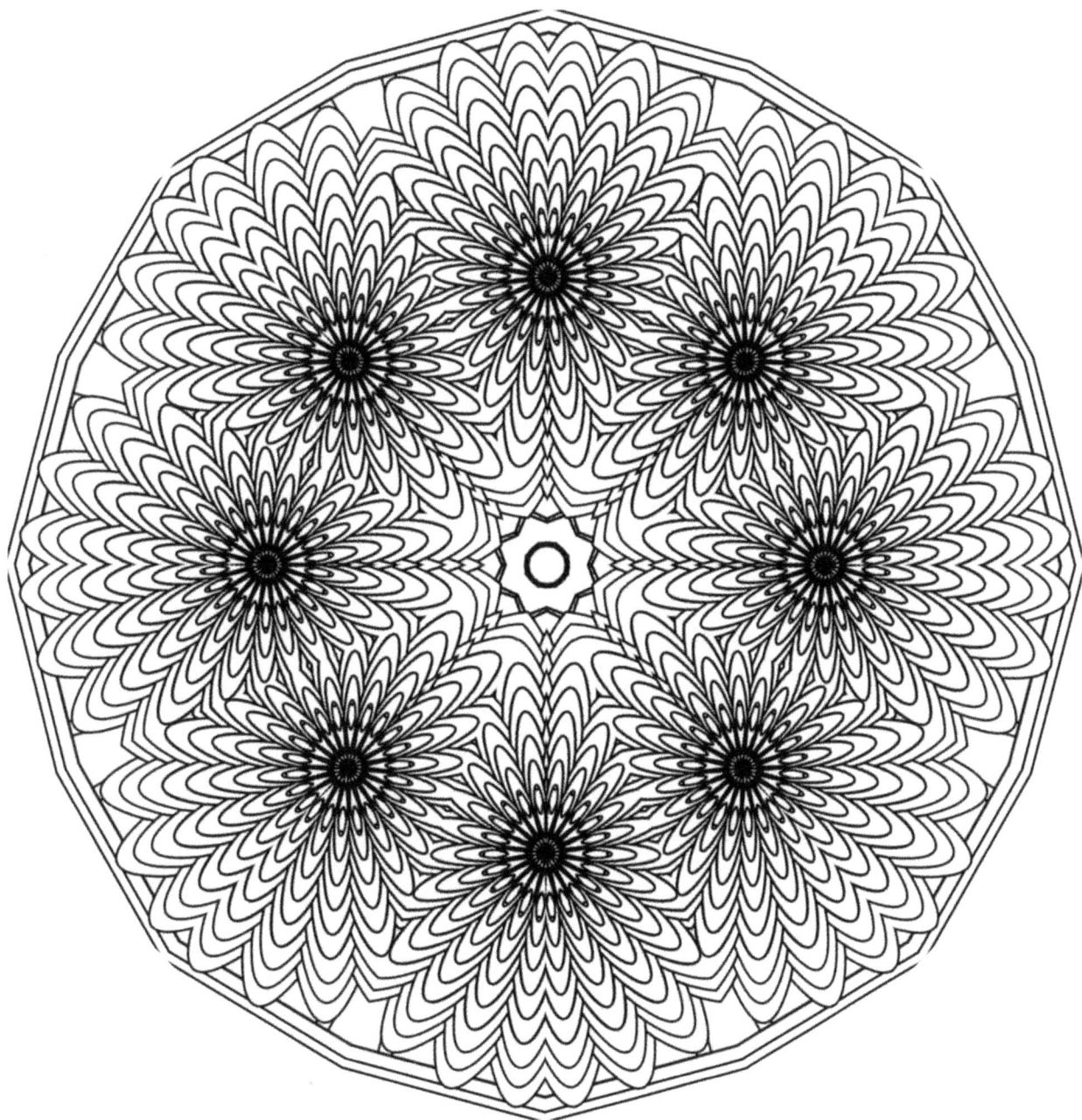

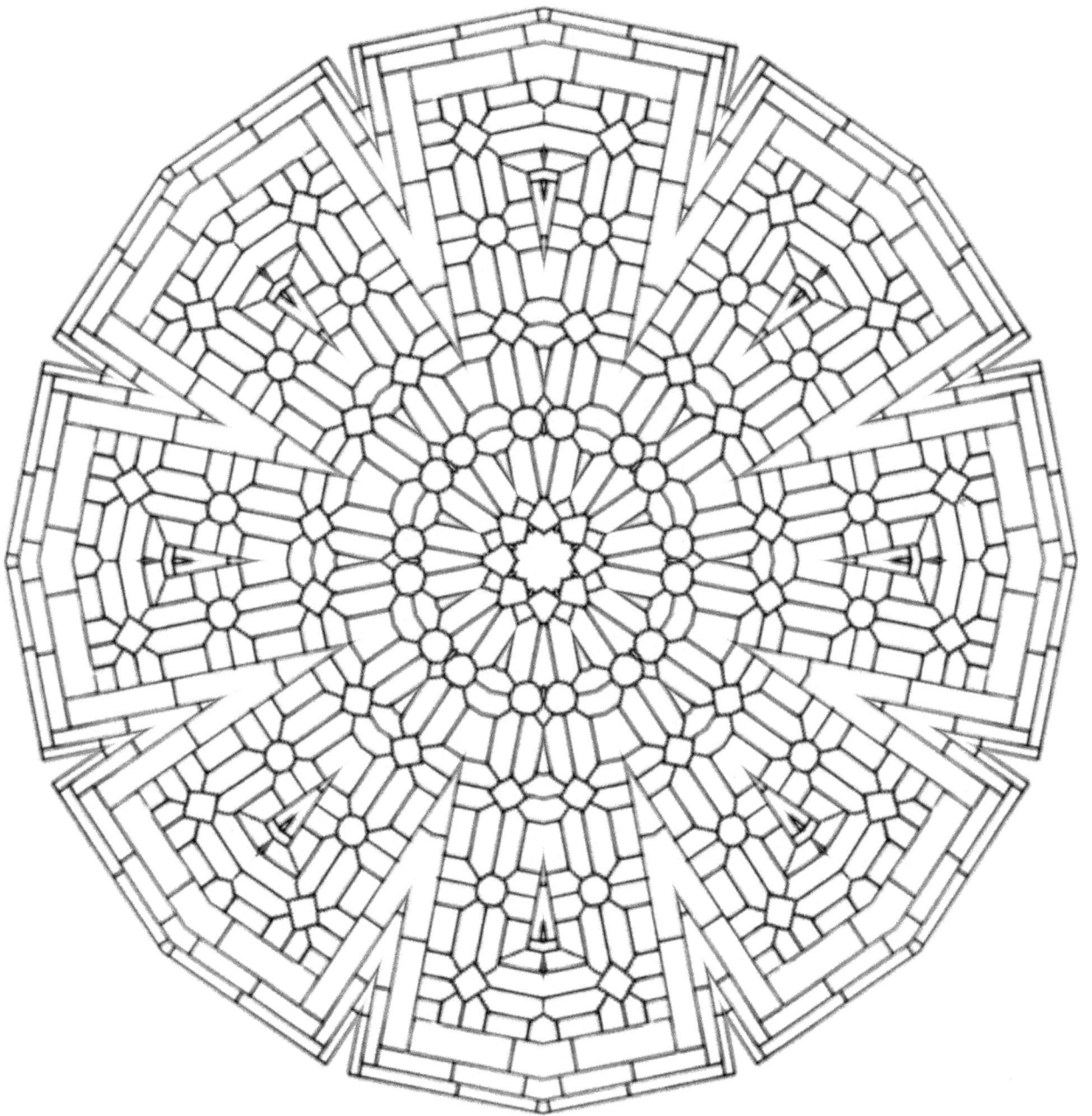

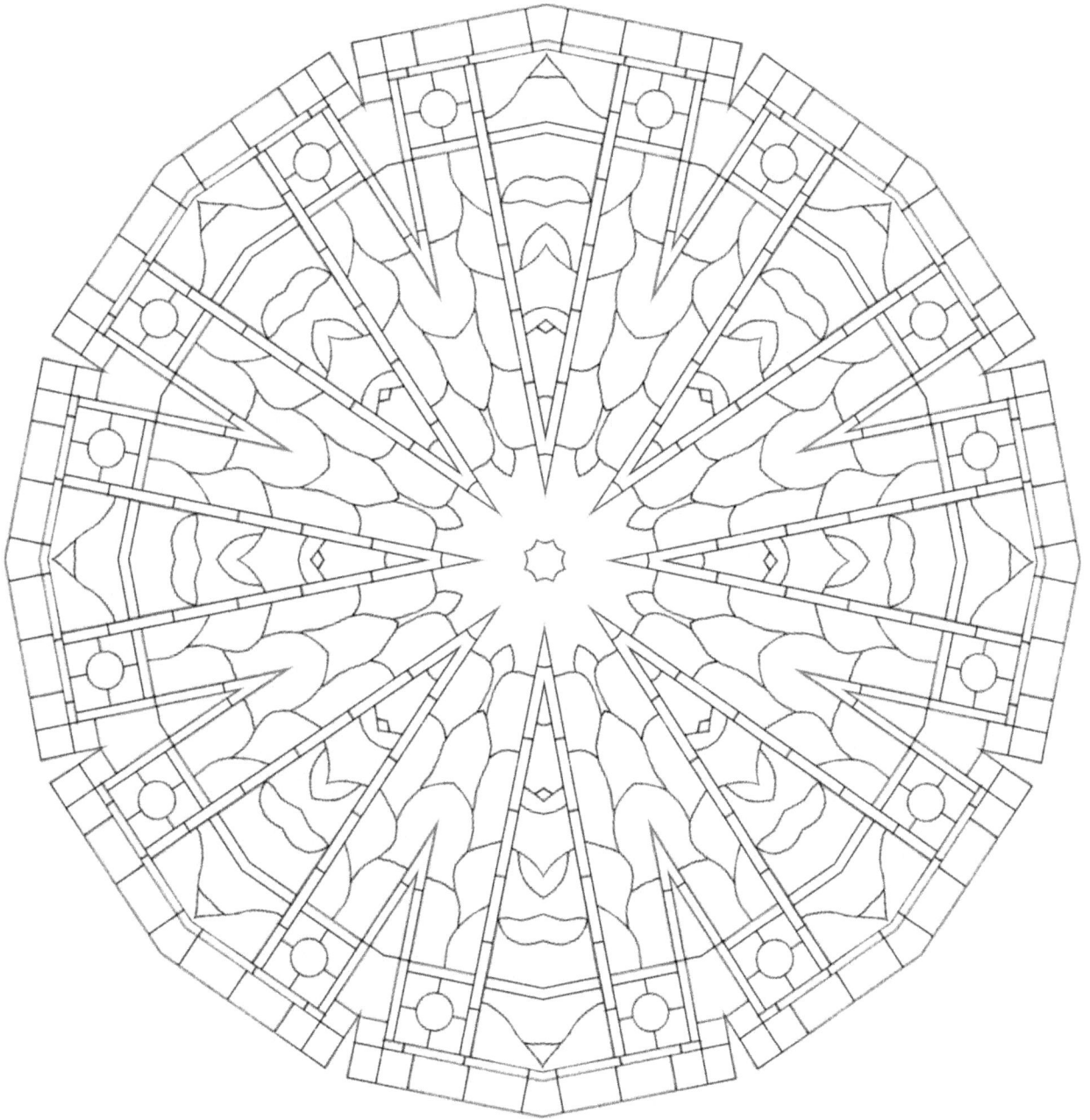

Notes

Notes

Blotter Page

Two blotter pages have been included for your convenience. Remove one or both and use them as a barrier between the page you are coloring and the next.

The designs in this book have been printed on one side of the page, but markers often bleed through even the best paper. To keep your art work pristine as you color and create, use another piece of paper as a buffer between the pages of this book, or use a thin piece of cardboard (cut one side from a cereal box, or use the thin cardboard insert that is found inside a new shirt)

Blotter Page

Two blotter pages have been included for your convenience. Remove one or both and use them as a barrier between the page you are coloring and the next.

The designs in this book have been printed on one side of the page, but markers often bleed through even the best paper. To keep your art work pristine as you color and create, use another piece of paper as a buffer between the pages of this book, or use a thin piece of cardboard (cut one side from a cereal box, or use the thin cardboard insert that is found inside a new shirt)

Thank you for buying a MandaLove Coloring Book!

♥

We've put together a FREE Bonus package of new mandalas, available for you to download at this link:

CreativeColoringBooksForAdults.SubscribeMeNow.com

♥

Join us on Facebook and take part in coloring contests and free book and supply give-aways. Show us your completed designs!

Facebook.com/CreativeColoringBooks

♥

Look for our coloring books on Amazon and at your local bookstore!

www.Amazon.com/author/CreativeColoringBooks

♥